T0128871

FAITH, PATRIOTISM AND LOVE POEMS

REMATA SUSEELA REDDY, Ph.D

Order this book online at www.trafford.com
or email orders@trafford.com

Most Trafford titles are also available at major online book retailers.

Print information available on the last page.

ISBN: 978-1-4907-7947-8 (sc)
ISBN: 978-1-4907-7946-1 (hc)
ISBN: 978-1-4907-7945-4 (e)

Library of Congress Control Number: 2016920366

Trafford rev. 03/04/2019

www.trafford.com
North America & international
toll-free: 1 888 232 4444 (USA & Canada)
fax: 812 355 4082

Princess Avanthi Reddy Remata

Dedicated to God and My Family

PREFACE

This poetry presents the poems the role that heredity places an important part in faith in God, patriotism and love. All poems speak in this book are original.

Faith is shown to imply an approbation of the will of God in requiring of us holiness and obedience, to the full measure of the perfection and spirituality demanded of us in the moral law. He appeals, in illustration of the obedience required, to the light of nature, and to the knowledge of good and evil which men enjoy through the law; but proves that without the light of saving faith there can be no adequate conception of the holiness required by the divine will, urging an acute distinction, which might rank as a separate contribution to the doctrine of conscience, and according to which its authority in determining the moral character of an action by no means implies the love of what is good, and the hatred of what is evil. The function of conscience he views is exclusively judicial, and shows that the motive which prompts to action must spring from other considerations. Two grounds are assigned on which faith approves of the holiness required of us:—the consistency of such a demand with the perfection of the divine nature; and its fitness, when full compliance is yielded with it, to advance us to the utmost perfection of which our own nature is capable.

Poems that salute the American Flag, speak out for freedom, and express gratitude and pride in those, past and present, who have served honorable and bravely to help make America a great country in which we live.

The love poems in this book are to be premier of the building blocks to discover, create and sustain a truly loving relationships with ourselves and one significant others. The poems I have shared in this book are always collection of my experiences.

Grateful acknowledgments are here made to those who helped while writing these poems. This work would not have reached its present form without their invaluable help. Finally, I want to thank my precious love to my beloved wife, Sathyavathi Remata. She gave me the valuable love and support for completion of this book.

CONTENTS

I. Faith Poems

PRAISE THE LORD:
A UNIVERSAL PRAYER

I don't know why I love you, O God

I don't know why I cry for you, O my Lord

Maybe you know…maybe you know.

Love me, allow me to love you!

O God, O my Lord, Jesus Christ, O my Savior

Love me, allow me to love you!

I love You with my whole heart,

All to thee Jesus! I surrender all! I surrender all!

You are the creator of the whole universe.

You are the cause of our existence.

And you are the word of living God.

You are dearer to us than our life.

You are the light of the world.

You are the abode of all and the holy spirit.

You are pure intelligence and the most acceptable.

You sacrificed to crucify and resurrected.

From the dead to wash our sins and save our lives.

You love the poorest of the poor.

You are kind, gracious and most merciful.

JESUS CHRIST

J-for- Joy in peace, love and truth;

say the people of the world

E-for- Everlasting heavenly father;

say the people of the world

S-for- Son of God, supreme soul;

say the people of the world

U-for-Universal light and knowledge;

say the people of the world

S-for- Supreme power and glory of

God; say the people of the world

C-for-Creator of the universe and

life; say the people of the world

H-for-Holy spirit and grace of God;

say the people of the world

R-for-Resurrection from the dead;

say the people of the world

I -for-Incarnation of God; say

the people of the world

S-for-Savior of the world and sinners;

say the people of the world

T-for-Trust in Jesus Christ forever;

say the people of the world

Jesus Christ is the Light of the World

Jesus Christ is the Living God

Jesus Christ is the Lord of Lords

Jesus Christ is the King of Kings

Jesus Christ is our Lord and Savior

Say the People of the World!

LORD OF LORDS!
KING OF KINGS

Oh Father, Lord of Lords, King

of Kings, Jesus Christ!

May the people of the world thank

thee for sprinkling the blessings,

and blessed the people touches

the lotus feet of the Lord.

Give us the love and strength to

always remember you,

and entertain you in our souls with

the utmost love and reverence.

Oh Father, Lord of Lords, King

of Kings, Jesus Christ!

May You keep the people of the

world in peace and happiness,

And, blessed, the people of the

world "glorify You Lord".

Come down to earth from the heaven

to save us from all evils and sins

and guide us to the righteous path,

to do only what is good.

SERVE THOU LORD

O Everlasting Father, Jesus Christ!

I don't ask any wealth from you

I don't have any wishes in my life

Let me always serve You, O Lord!

O Everlasting Father, Jesus Christ!

I have faith in You for eternal life

You are gracious to purify my soul

Let me always serve You, O Lord!

O Everlasting Father, Jesus Christ!

I am blind; I can't see You

I am lame; I can't walk to You

Let me always serve You, O Lord!

O Everlasting Father, Jesus Christ!

Take me from the darkness to the light

Change my life and grant me salvation

Let me always serve You, O Lord!

HIS NAME IS JESUS CHRIST

O Mother, I have seen today a Holy Man

He is so beautiful and gracious

everybody is saying; "He is incarnation of God"

O Mother, His name is Jesus Christ.

O Mother, I have seen today a Heavenly Man

He is the Man of truth and wisdom

everybody is saying; "He is God

from the true God"

O Mother, His name is Jesus Christ.

O Mother, I have seen today a Shepherd Man

He is the Man of peace and love

everybody is saying; "He is light of the World"

O Mother, His name is Jesus Christ.

O Mother, I have seen today a Saintly Man

He is all perfect and the supreme soul

everybody is saying; "He is light of the World"

O Mother, His name is Jesus Christ.

The Poor Soul

My soul called so many times, He never speaks

I asked every soul of the World,

whereabouts of Him,

Everybody saying, "He is the Son of God,

He is the child of Mother Mary,

His name is Jesus Christ".

O Jesus! I brought the holy waters

from the mighty oceans

to wash your lotus feet, fall on

your feet and surrender all;

I brought the sacred waters from the holy rivers

to give you a splendid bath and

cleansing all my sins.

This poor soul waited very long

time for you to come

my eyes are swollen crying for you, O God!

I don't know how long I can

wait, maybe you know,

that day will come very soon, standing

on the promises of God.

O Jesus! Welcome to this sweet

home and touch this poor soul

I know you are so hungry and it's

the time for the supper,

I made sweet feast with bread, wine

and fruits for you to eat.

I know you are so tired and it's

the time for you to sleep,

I made a beautiful bed in this

splendid full moon light.

I don't know whether I will be

born again to serve you,

Let this poor soul serve you O

Lord, till my last breath.

O God! Fill My Heart

When the morning sun rises in the east

When the evening sun sets in the west

When I sprinkle the holy water cleansing my sins

When I do morning prayers with peace of mind

When I share a piece of bread with my family

When I am at work whole day with stress

When I rejoice serving the Lord and the people

I always remember my Holy Father, "Jesus Christ"

O God! Fill my heart with joy, peace and love.

When I suffer at times from the poverty

When I fall sick and have no hopes to recover

When I do sins knowingly and unknowingly

When I visit the holy temple for Sunday Worship

When I read the Holy Bible

with faith for salvation

When Santa Clause appears on Christmas Eve

When the children sing "Jingle bell Jingle bell"

I always remember my Holy Father, "Jesus Christ"

O God! Fill my heart with joy, peace and love

CHANT THY NAME

O People of the world!

Chant thy Name through "Jesus Christ"

Thy name is sweet and powerful

the sweetest name that I know

Thy Jesus thy Jesus! Jesus Jesus thy thy!

Thy Christ thy Christ! Christ Christ thy thy!

I want to bring the flowers for the worship

O Jesus! You turned into the flowers

I want to bring the lights in to the darkness

O Jesus! You turned in to the lights

You are the light of the World

and word of living God

You are everywhere and in

every soul of the World

Chant thy Name through "Jesus Christ"

Thy Jesus thy Jesus! Jesus Jesus thy thy!

Thy Christ thy Christ! Christ Christ thy thy!

I want to bring the water for cleansing sins

O Jesus! You turned in to the holy waters

I want to bring the foods for the poor

O Jesus you turned in to the mighty foods

You love the poorest of the poor

and word of living god

You are everywhere and in

every soul of the World

Chant thy Name through "Jesus Christ"

Thy Jesus thy Jesus! Jesus Jesus thy thy!

Thy Christ thy Christ! Christ Christ thy thy!

For thine is the power and the glory

Sprit of God descend upon our hearts

Save our sins forever and ever

Thy kingdom comes on earth from heaven

Chant thy Name through "Jesus Christ"

Thy Jesus thy Jesus! Jesus Jesus thy thy!

Thy Christ thy Christ! Christ Christ thy thy!

Universal Meditation

Oh the son of God! Jesus Christ,

salutations to thee

Oh the child of virgin mother! Jesus

Christ, salutations to thee

Oh the king of Israel! Jesus

Christ, salutations to thee

Oh the prince of peace! Jesus

Christ, salutations to thee!

Oh the creator of the universe! Jesus

Christ, salutations to thee

Oh the light of the World! Jesus

Christ, salutations to thee

Oh the king of Emanuel, Jesus

Christ, salutations to thee

Oh the father of love! Jesus

Christ, salutations to thee!

Oh the lord of beginning! Jesus

Christ, salutations to thee

Oh the word of living God! Jesus

Christ, salutations to thee

Oh the savior of sinners! Jesus

Christ, salutations to thee

Oh the lord of Holy Sprit! Jesus

Christ, salutations to thee!

Oh the lord of truth! Jesus

Christ, salutations to thee

Oh the lord of salvation! Jesus

Christ, salutations to thee

Oh the lord of everything! Jesus

Christ, salutations to thee

Oh the lord of Lords! Jesus

Christ, salutations to thee!

Oh the Christ of God! Jesus

Christ, salutations to thee

Oh the Lamb of God! Jesus

Christ, salutations to thee

Oh the eternal Father of heaven!

Jesus Christ, salutations to thee

Oh the God of thy Father! Jesus

Christ, salutations to thee!

Oh the Lion of Judah! Jesus

Christ, salutations to thee

Oh the Author of Life! Jesus

Christ, salutations to thee

Oh the Teacher of God! Jesus

Christ, salutations to thee

Oh the Head of the Church! Jesus

Christ, salutations to thee!

Oh the Bright Morning Star! Jesus

Christ, salutations to thee

Oh the Holy and Righteousness!

Jesus Christ, salutations to thee

Oh the Word of God, Jesus

Christ, salutations to thee

Oh the father of love! Jesus

Christ, salutations to thee!

Oh the king of kings! Jesus

Christ, salutations to thee

Oh the lamb of God! Jesus

Christ, salutations to thee

Oh the son of David! Jesus

Christ, salutations to thee

Oh the lord of Holy Sprit! Jesus

Christ, salutations to thee!

Oh the lord of Righteousness! Jesus

Christ, salutations to thee

Oh the author of Life! Jesus

Christ, salutations to thee

Oh the bright morning Star! Jesus

Christ, salutations to thee

Oh the eternal father! Jesus

Christ, salutations to thee!

Oh the mighty Lord! Jesus

Christ, salutations to thee

Oh the wonderful Advisor! Jesus

Christ, salutations to thee

Oh the head of the Church! Jesus

Christ, salutations to thee

Oh the son of Man! Jesus Christ,
salutations to thee!

Oh, the blood of Jesus! Jesus
Christ, salutations to thee
Oh the resurrection and Life! Jesus
Christ, salutations to thee
Oh the king of Israel! Jesus
Christ, salutations to thee
Oh the prince of peace! Jesus
Christ, salutations to thee!

Oh the creator of the universe! Jesus
Christ, salutations to thee
Oh the light of the World! Jesus
Christ, salutations to thee
Oh the king of Emanuel, Jesus
Christ, salutations to thee

Oh the father of love! Jesus

Christ, salutations to thee!

Oh the lord of beginning! Jesus

Christ, salutations to thee

Oh the word of living God! Jesus

Christ, salutations to thee

Oh the savior of sinners! Jesus

Christ, salutations to thee

Oh the lord of Holy Sprit! Jesus

Christ, salutations to thee!

Oh the lord of truth! Jesus

Christ, salutations to thee

Oh the lord of salvation! Jesus

Christ, salutations to thee

Oh the lord of everything! Jesus

Christ, salutations to thee

Oh the lord of Lords! Jesus
Christ, salutations to thee!

Oh the lord of truth! Jesus
Christ, salutations to thee
Oh the lord of salvation! Jesus
Christ, salutations to thee
Oh the lord of everything! Jesus
Christ, salutations to thee
Oh the lord of Lords! Jesus
Christ, salutations to thee

Oh the Lion of Judah! Jesus
Christ, salutations to thee
Oh the Author of Life! Jesus
Christ, salutations to thee
Oh the Teacher of God! Jesus
Christ, salutations to thee

Oh the Head of the Church! Jesus

Christ, salutations to thee!

Oh the Bright Morning Star! Jesus

Christ, salutations to thee

Oh the Holy and Righteousness!

Jesus Christ, salutations to thee

Oh the Word of God, Jesus

Christ, salutations to thee

Oh the father of love! Jesus

Christ, salutations to thee!

Oh the king of kings! Jesus

Christ, salutations to thee

Oh the Lamb of God! Jesus

Christ, salutations to thee

Oh the son of David! Jesus

Christ, salutations to thee

Oh the lord of Holy Spirit! Jesus

Christ, salutations to thee!

Oh the lord of Righteousness! Jesus

Christ, salutations to thee

Oh the author of Life! Jesus

Christ, salutations to thee

Oh the bright morning Star! Jesus

Christ, salutations to thee

Oh the eternal father! Jesus

Christ, salutations to thee!

Om the mighty Lord! Jesus

Christ, salutations to thee

Oh the wonderful Advisor! Jesus

Christ, salutations to thee

Oh the head of the Church! Jesus

Christ, salutations to thee

Oh the son of Man! Jesus Christ,

salutations to thee!

Oh, the blood of Jesus! Jesus

Christ, salutations to thee

Oh the resurrection and Life! Jesus

Christ, salutations to thee

Oh the king of Israel! Jesus

Christ, salutations to thee

Oh the prince of peace! Jesus

Christ, salutations to thee!

Oh the creator of the universe! Jesus

Christ, salutations to thee

Oh the light of the World! Jesus

Christ, salutations to thee

Oh the king of Emanuel, Jesus

Christ, salutations to thee

Oh the father of love! Jesus
Christ, salutations to thee!

Oh the lord of beginning! Jesus
Christ, salutations to thee
Oh the word of living God! Jesus
Christ, salutations to thee
Oh the savior of sinners! Jesus
Christ, salutations to thee
Oh the lord of Holy Spirit! Jesus
Christ, salutations to thee!

Oh the lord of truth! Jesus
Christ, salutations to thee
Oh the lord of salvation! Jesus
Christ, salutations to thee
Oh the lord of everything! Jesus
Christ, salutations to thee

Oh the lord of Lords! Jesus
Christ, salutations to thee!

Oh the lord of Almighty! Jesus
Christ, salutations to thee
Oh the lord of Beloved Son! Jesus
Christ, salutations to thee
Oh the lord of Christ of God! Jesus
Christ, salutations to thee
Oh the lord Mighty God! Jesus
Christ, salutations to thee!

AWESOME GOD

Awesome God beautiful! Awesome God merciful!

God is calling me to follow His Son, Holy Ghost

God is awakening me to serve the Lord with faith

Holy Father and His Son Jesus Christ is one God

Go around the World! Praise the Lord

His name is so sweet, sweet and powerful

Chant Thy name through Jesus

Christ for salvation

Jesus Christ! Jesus Christ! Jesus Christ!

Sunday morning worship time

in the Holy Temple

I bow my knees kissing the lotus feet of the Lord

Closing my eyes and asking for the Hope

While the Universe and the World rejoicing

My sins are cleansed and wishes are fulfilled

Blessed the poor soul with joy, peace and love

My joy of love has no bounds

to reach the Holy Sprit

Rejoice serving the Lord forever

with utmost reverence

Tell the World, Jesus Christ is

the light of the World

He is the word of living God and savior of sinners

He is the Lord of Lords! He is the King of Kings!

His name is so sweet, sweet and powerful

Chant Thy name through Jesus

Christ for salvation

Jesus Christ! Jesus Christ! Jesus Christ!

I LOVE JESUS

When I look at the rising sun, I see Jesus

When I look at the setting sun, I see Jesus

When I look at the twinkling stars, I see Jesus

When I look at the splendid full moon, I see Jesus

When I look at the mighty oceans, I see Jesus

When I look at the snowy mountains, I see Jesus

When I look at the green rain forests, I see Jesus

Jesus is the only begotten son of God

I love Jesus! I love Jesus! I love Jesus!

When I look at the newborn babies, I see Jesus

When I look at the poorest of the poor, I see Jesus

When I visit the holy temples, I see Jesus

When I look at the holy cross, I see Jesus

When I read the holy bible, I see Jesus

When I think of Santa Clause, I see Jesus

When I celebrate the Christmas Day, I see Jesus

Jesus is everywhere and in every soul of the world

I love Jesus! I love Jesus! I love Jesus!

MY DAILY PRAYERS

O Father! Son of God! Jesus Christ! O My Savior!

I thank you O Lord! For

providing food and shelter,

Please come down to help the people of the world,

the people of the world need your blessings.

Bless us so much with prosperity, hale and healthy,

Keep the world in peace and happiness,

Help the poorest of the poor,

and Help them who helped my family and me.

Please give me the strength, love,

peace and happiness,

always to remember you with utmost reverence,

and to serve the Lord and people of the world,

Please stay in our hearts and safeguard

from all evils and sins,

In the name of "Jesus", AMEN!

ALWAYS REMEMBER JESUS CHRIST

Joy comes from the contentment

Energy comes from the supreme soul

Strength comes from the heavenly father

Universal truth comes from the courage

Success comes from the hard work

Creativity comes from the knowledge

Holiness comes from the love

Righteousness comes from the self

Inner strength comes from the peace of mind

Salvation comes from the devotion to God

Trust comes from the worship Jesus Christ!

Jesus Christ is our Lord

Jesus Christ is our Father

Jesus Christ is our Savior

Always remember Jesus Christ!

LITTLE JESUS

Little, little Jesus, sweet little Jesus
Holy child Jesus, light of the world Jesus
Son of God Jesus, child of Mary Jesus
Beautiful Jesus! Little, little Jesus!

Little, little Jesus, sweet little Jesus
Awesome God Jesus, little angel Jesus
Kingdom of heaven Jesus, holy sprit Jesus
Beautiful Jesus! Little, little Jesus!

Little, little Jesus, sweet little Jesus
Glory, glory Jesus, righteousness Jesus
Joy and peace Jesus, love and truth Jesus
Beautiful Jesus! Little, little Jesus!

Little, little Jesus, sweet little Jesus

Twinkle, twinkle Jesus, little star Jesus

King of Kings Jesus, Lord of Lord Jesus

Beautiful Jesus! Little, little Jesus!

Go O Boy GO

Go O Boy Go! Go and see the crazy world!
No one knows you are an orphan
God only knows that you are his child.

Go O Boy Go! Go and see the crazy world!
Don't be afraid moving forward
Don't be ashamed telling the world you are poor
Keep faith in Lord Jesus Christ
Lord shall open the doors and
give you the eternal life.

Go O Boy Go! Go and see the crazy world!
Never commit the sins knowingly
Share the love with Lord Jesus
Seek always God's grace
Lord shall provide you joy and peace
And shall give you the salvation.

MERRY CHRISTMAS

Here comes Christmas! Here comes Christmas!

Jesus was born; gave the light to the world

The whole world rejoiced and everyone's

Heart is filled with joy, peace and love

Lift the Lord Jesus; Glorify the Lord Christ

Sing the Christmas song, Jingle bell; Jingle bell

Praise the Lord "Jesus Christ",

Here comes Christmas! Merry Christmas!

Here comes Christmas! Here comes Christmas!

Jesus was born; spoke the truth to people

The whole world is delighted and everyone's

House is decorated with Christmas Trees

Lift the Lord Jesus; Glorify the Lord Christ

Sing the Christmas song, Jingle bell; Jingle bell

Praise the Lord "Jesus Christ",

Here comes the Christmas! Merry Christmas!

Blessed this poor home and family

Shines the light and peace on earth

Come and worship, Come and worship

Worship Christ the new born King

Lift the Lord Jesus; Glorify the Lord Christ

Sing the Christmas song, Jingle bell; Jingle bell

Praise the Lord "Jesus Christ",

Here comes the Christmas! Merry Christmas!

Faith in God

Nature created fears in the hearts

of people of America

It was a curse that nature has raged America

Hurricane Katrina and Hurricane Irene

And a tropical cyclone Lee

slammed the Gulf Coast

And East Coast of America with torrential rains,

Storm surges, Floods and tornadoes that caused

Deaths and billion dollars property damages

People have no hopes, but have faith in God

Peace, peace and peace be with

us, "People of America"

After math, God has given

strength and hope to the

President Obama, federal, State and local officials

And the people of America to rebuild the America

People understand everything

that God has a purpose

They have prayers with tears, but have faith

Peace, peace and peace be with

us. "People of America"

The Bible
(Source: Holy Bible-by the
Gideons International)

And said, truly I say to you, except you be converted, and become as little children, you shall not enter into the kingdom of heaven.

Matthew 18:

But without faith it is impossible to please him: for he that comes to God must believe that he is, and that he is a rewarder of them that diligently seek him.

Hebrews 11:6

But seek you first the kingdom of God, and his righteousness; and all these things shall be added to you.

Matthew 6:33

Seek God's will in all that You do He will direct your path.

Proverbs 3:6

Let all that you do be done in Love.

1 Corinthians 16:14

DONOT FEAR for I am with You.

Isaiah 41:10

Casting all your anxieties on him, because he cares for you.

1 Peter 5:7

Come to me, all who labor and are heavy laden, and I will give you rest.

Matthew 11.28

It is better to take refuge in the Lord than to trust in Man.

Psalm 118:8

Be strong, and let your heart take courage, all you who wait for Lord

Psalm 31:24

Peace I leave with you; my peace I give it you, not as the world gives do I give it to you. Let not your hearts be troubled, neither let them be afraid.

John 14:27

Restore to me the joy of your salvation, and uphold me willing spirit.

Psalm 51:32

If we say we have no sin, we deceive ourselves, and the truth is not in us. If we confess our sins, he is faithful and just forgive us our sins and to cleanse us from all unrighteousness.

1 John 1:8, 9

Have mercy on me, O God, according to your steadfast love; according to your abundant mercy blot out my transgressions.

Psalm 51:1

For God so loved the World, that he gave his only son, that whoever believes in him should not perish but have eternal life.

John 3:16

A Prayer

Dear God, I confess that I have sinned and done wrong, I believe that your Son, Jesus Christ took the punishment.

II. Patriotism Poems

MAY GOD BLESS AMERICA

America is the land of United States

America is the land of immigrants

America is the land of democracy

May God bless America.

America is the land of liberty

America is the land of integrity

America is the land of sovereignty

May God bless America.

America is the land of love

America is the land of peace

America is the land of resources

May God bless America.

America is the land of patriotism

America is the land of soldiery

America is the land of opportunity

May God bless America.

GEORGE WALKER BUSH!
HONORABLE PRESIDENT
OF AMERICA

G -Glory and grace of God

and God bless America

E -Energetic and powerful commander in chief

O -Omnipotent establishing righteousness,

democracy and freedom

R -Republican Forty Third

President of the United States

G -Gracious spirit of the Governor of Texas

E -Evangelist for Universal peace,

love, truth and wisdom

W -World's the most popular President of America

A -America united in Twenty First

century leading the faith

L -Leader for compassionate conservatism

K -Kind-hearted,hospitable,cheerful,

Patriot and well liked President

E -Everlasting American President

in American History

R -Rejoice serving the Lord and

the People of America

B -Blessed with the Fist Lady Laura

Welch Bush and twin daughters

U -Universal prayer for liberty, integrity

and sovereignty of America

S -Supreme power securing and

liberating the people of America

H -Honorable President of America!

George Walker Bush!

Barak Hussain OBAMA! Honorable President of America

B-Barack Obama, the first Black President

of United States of America

A-American forty fourth Democratic

President of the United States

B- Blessed with First Lady Michel Obama

and two loving beautiful daughters

R-Ring a Ring o' Roses, a pocket full

o' posies, Atishoo, we all fall down

A- America united in twenty first century

leading faith, wisdom and strong

C-Considers himself the most gracious

merciful man in the world

K-Kind, Loving Person and create a

stronger future for our country

H-Hail, hail to the commander-in-chief of United States of America

U-Universal Love, Light and Knowledge for one God, one Nation

S- Supreme power and glory of God; say the people of the world

S- Superman securing and liberating the people of America

E- Evangelist for Universal peace, love, truth and wisdom

I-In the name of Allah, the All-beneficent, the All- kind and merciful

N-National Leader for freedom, health care and World's terrorism

O-Omnipotent establishing righteousness, democracy and freedom

B-Blessed the poor soul with joy, peace and love

A-America is the land of patriotism,

America is the land of beautiful

M-Man of courage, peace, patriotic, faith

in god, love in American people

A-America united in Twenty First century

leading the faith, patriotism, love

A MESSAGE FROM GOD

God descends on to the earth since

ages to destroy the evils

And establish his Kingdom and

righteousness and peace.

God created the Heaven, the Earth, and the Life

For God, there is no religion,

caste, creed and color.

God loves his children so much and saves

them from sufferings, evils and sins.

God was waiting long time for the September

Eleventh an historical event of America.

On this day, the evils destroyed the two great

towers in the beautiful city of New York

And killed the innocent children of God;

whose souls may be in rest and peace.

God chose his child George W. Bush, The

President of America to carry his Mission

And to destroy the evils and bring the

justice to the people of America.

The President Bush is blessed with the

strength, the courage and the long life

The Government, the people of America

and the World united and supported

The President George Bush with the

utmost reverence and trust.

Under his super power, the heroes and

brave solders of America are hunting

The evils from cave to cave and destroying

the cells of the evil acts of the world

A message from God: The President

George Bush shall complete the

God's Mission during his tenure of the

Eight Year Term to destroy the evils

And establish the righteousness, global

peace and rejoice the people of America

III. LOVE POEMS

HELLO DEAR! MY DEAR!

Who are you to reach my heart

and smile in my life

Just today, I recognize that, yes, your name is love

When love at first sight, you look

so young and beautiful

When I look at your naughty eyes,

I don't get sleep at night

When I see your sweet lips, I feel kissing you

So sorry say to you that I love you,

I love you, I love you, Hello Dear! My Dear!

When the night is full of moonlight,

I see you in my dreams

When the day is full of busy, I miss you so much

When I see your beautiful body,

I feel hugging you

So sorry say to you that I love you,

I love you, I love you, Hello Dear! My Dear!

When I send you a love gift, I see

you in happy tears and smile

When the winter comes with full of

snow white, I see you in shy

When the spring blooms with full

of red roses, I feel dating you

So sorry say to you that I love you,

I love you, I love you, Hello Dear! My Dear!

JUST LIKE THAT

I want to tell you something, just like that

I want to ask you something, just like that

When my heart feelings slip my lips

That's the hug, that's the kiss, that's the love

Just like that, Just like that, just like that!

Everybody saying, you are so beautiful

Somebody saying, you are an angel, O baby

I don't know whereabouts you to

send the love the message

I fly from Louisiana to Chicago to Niagara Falls

Where the lovebirds are meeting!

Everybody saying, you are a wonderful girl

Somebody saying, you are my sweet heart, O baby

I don't know where I am going

to look for your love

I fly from California to Mississippi

to Washington D.C.

Where the sweet dreams come true!

Everybody saying, the life is too short

Somebody saying, the love is crazy, O baby

I don't know why you are waiting

for us to enjoy the life

I fly from New York to London to Paris

where the great lovers are meeting!

LOVE MESSAGE

Let my heart beats with sound of music

Let the oceans sing and the clouds rain

With thunder and lightning

To send the love message

That I am in love with you

Love is sweet and eternal!

Let the sweet dreams come true

Let the stars twinkle and angels sing

To send the love message

That I am in love with you

Love is great and unforgetful.

Let the flowers bloom in sunshine

Let my tears flow and the winds blow

With tenderness to send the love message

That I am in love with you

Love is true and passionate.

MY EYES ARE TELLING

My eyes are telling that I love you

my lips are telling that I kiss you

Love is blind; Kiss is sweet

Love Kiss! Love Kiss! Love Kiss!

Beautiful! You are so beautiful

you are my heart; you are my dream

Life is too short, don't waste our time baby

every day, every night, Let us enjoy come on!

Crazy World! Let us have a drink baby

When I drink, everybody drinks and dance

When I sing, everybody rocks and shakes

don't care this world; Let us enjoy come on!

Any body from you, don't ask what for

In this age all these feelings are crazy

I love you so much, I like you very much

Every day, every night, Let us enjoy come on!

O MY LOVE

One clear night, in moon light,

I saw a beautiful girl

standing on the banks of the Mississippi river

her eyes are blinking! Her lips are smiling!

Asking for my love, O my love!

O my love! O my love!

One clear night, in moon light

I saw her smiling in my sweet dreams

I can't imagine! An angel comes from the heaven

reaching my heart with abundance of love

her eyes are hugging; her lips are kissing

asking for my love, O my love!

O my love! O my love!

One clear night, in moon light

I saw her standing on the beaches

of the Ocean springs,

I can't imagine! Somebody walks in to my life

reaching my heart with abundance of love

her eyes are crying; her lips are begging

asking for my love, O my love!

O my love! O my love!

WELCOME TO MY LOVE

Sometimes, I told welcome to my first love

Just today, I told welcome to my second love

In my first love, I saw the sweetness

I saw the honeyness in my second love

Love, love, my first love! Love,

love, my second love!

At far, I hear the sounds of the lightning thunders

Bringing so many remembrances of my first love

At dawn, the nightingale sings the love songs

Rejoice the love birds of my second love

Romeo and Juliet's, the first love; my

wife, and me the second love

Love, love, my first love! Love,

love, my second love!

In the night, the sweet dreams smile on her lips

I kiss my sweet heart of my first love

Up in the sky, the splendid full moon light

I hug my beautiful wife of my second love

Love is mad in my first love; love

is great in my second love

Love, love, my first love! Love,

love, my second love!

WHEREABOUTS OF MY DEAR

The day is looking for the night

The night is looking for the moonlight

My heart is looking for my dear

Somewhere, some times I saw her

Ever since I am in love with her

I sent the love message

Through the woods, through the clouds,

Through the birds and through the

Roaring Winds, my eyes are swollen for

long waiting of my dear And hoping

That she will come back soon

I looked all over the world and

I asked all the people of the world,

whereabouts of my dear, every body is

saying that she is sleeping in My heart

My heart is filled with Joy,

But I can't see her forever

O Mother Moon! Beautiful dear!

Tell me please whereabouts of my dear.

HAPPY BIRTH DAY

I have come for you

brought so many remembrances

with love and blessings

Oh Dear! Happy birth day to you!

Somewhere, sometimes I saw you

Ever since I am in love with You

Love is great and unforgettable

I love you with all my heart

I remember you! I remember you!

Oh Dear! Happy birth day to you!

I don't know this everlasting bondage

Why I love and like you so much

Maybe You look so young and beautiful

Like an angel in the heaven

You have stolen my heart

Love is eternal and passionate

I love You! You love me!

Oh Dear! Happy birth day to you!

HAPPY, HAPPY, HAPPY

I see my dream girl, Happy

She is beautiful girl, Happy

She smiles at me, Happy

Her eyes whispers, Happy

I kiss her sweet lips, Happy

My heart loves her, Happy

I hug my Sweetheart, Happy

When I date her, Happy

When I engage her, Happy

When I marry her, Happy

When I become Dad, Happy

Happy! Happy! Happy!

LOVE

Love mom and dad who gave you birth

Love grandpa and grandma who are God fathers

Love wife and husband who are the bondage

Love brothers and sisters who are siblings

Love your teacher, that's where you get knowledge

Love your motherland where you took birth

Love your friends who always stand with you

Love your relatives with whom you always enjoy

Love your nabors in whom God lives

Love the nature who gives you shelter,

Love the supreme soul who is within you

Love everything, that's where God loves you

Love Jesus Christ from whom you

receive love, peace and grace

My Love is Awesome

We were true friends in high school
In college life we love each other
That love was something! Something!
My love is awesome and unforgettable.

Seasons changed, years passed
Still I remember that love
That love is great and unforgettable
My love is awesome and unforgettable.

We will born again for each other
And, we are made for each other
That love is sweet and joyful
My love is awesome and unforgettable.

THE LOVE IS TRUE

Stars are falling from the sky

telling the love is true

The moon is saying Go and kiss my sweetheart

Love is beautiful, but she is no more in this world

Love is true, Love is true, and the Love is true.

Tears are falling from heaven

telling the love is true

The love is saying Go and hug my sweetheart

Love is beautiful, but she is no more in this world

Love is true, Love is true, and the Love is true.

Rains are falling from the clouds

telling the love is true

The rainbow is saying Go and kiss my sweetheart

Love is beautiful, but she is no more in this world

Love is true, Love is true, and the Love is true.

Memorial Prayer

God, the Father of Heaven, God, the

Son, Redeemer of the world

God, the Holy Spirit, Jesus Christ

Holy Trinity, One God

Holy Mary, Holy Mother of God,

Holy Virgin of virgins,

Mother of Christ,

Mother of divine grace,

Mother of Peace.

Have mercy on us in memory

of our beloved daughter

who rests in peace in heaven

(Repeat at the end of each phrase)

O Lord

You are the creator of the whole universe

You are the cause of our existence

And you are the word of living God

You are everywhere and in

every soul of the World.

Amen.

O Lord

You are dearer to us than our life

You are the light of the world

You are the abode of all and the holy spirit

You are pure intelligence and the most acceptable

Amen

O Lord

You sacrificed to crucify and resurrected

From the dead to wash our sins and save our lives

You love the poorest of the poor

You are kind, gracious and most merciful.

Amen

For thine is the power and the glory

Spirit of God descend upon our hearts

Thy kingdom comes on earth from heaven

Save our sins forever and ever

Amen.

Our Father, who art in heaven,

Thy kingdom come on to the earth

Give us this day our daily bread

and the power, and the glory, forever.

Amen.

I WANT TO FOLLOW!
FOLLOW! FOLLOW YOU!

I Want to Follow! Follow! Follow You

I Want to Follow! Follow! Follow You

I Want to Follow! Follow! Follow You

Chic Bhuma! Chic Bhuma! Chic Bhuma!

Boom Chicca! Boom Chicca! Boom Chicca!

Ye! Ye! Ye! Oh! Oh! Oh!

Mama tells grab the baby as I like it

Papa tells love the baby as I like it

Sheila tells chase the baby as I like it

Lora tells take the baby wherever I want to be

To the East; to the West; to the

North; to the South!

Take the baby around the world

Make the baby so crazy and sexy

I Want to Follow! Follow! Follow You

I Want to Follow! Follow! Follow You

I Want to Follow! Follow! Follow You

Baby! You know I am just sweet sixteen

O sweet heart! I waited so long for you to come

Now this is the time for you to hug and kiss me

Mama tells hug the baby as I like it

Papa tells kiss the baby as I like it

Sheila tells shake the baby as I like it

Lora tells take the baby wherever I want to be

To the East; to the West; to the

North; to the South!

Take the baby around the world

Make the baby so crazy and sexy

I Want to Follow! Follow! Follow You

I Want to Follow! Follow! Follow You

I Want to Follow! Follow! Follow You

Wow! beautiful eyes! Baby Stare in to my eyes

O sweet heart! You are so beautiful!

I love you so much baby

look at beautiful Hubby dimple cheeks

Baby when you are ready for me to hug and kiss

Mama tells love the baby as I like it

Papa tells kiss the baby as like it

Sheila tells shake the baby as I like it

Lora tells take the baby wherever I want to be

To the East; to the West; to the

North; to the South!

Take the baby around the world

Make the baby so crazy and sexy

I Want to Follow! Follow! Follow You

I Want to Follow! Follow! Follow You

I Want to Follow! Follow! Follow You

DR. REMATA SUSEELA REDDY

Dr. Reddy was born in India and migrated to USA 1n 1989 and subsequently became USA citizen. Dr. Reddy served as a scientist in Government of India and Canada for more than twenty years and then joined at Jackson State University in 1994.Within the Department of Physics and Atmospheric Sciences and Geoscience at Jackson

State University, Dr. Reddy, Associate Professor of Meteorology, is responsible for teaching a variety of undergraduate and graduate courses. His teaching and research interests include Meteorology/Climatology, Remote Sensing and Satellite Meteorology and Numerical Modeling. Dr. Reddy is associated with NASA, NOAA and NSF funded projects investigating education and research in meteorology/ climatology. Reddy has published numerous papers in the areas of meteorology and climatology. He has participated and presented papers in national and international conferences/meetings. Dr. Reddy has interests in poetry and his poems have received the best poet awards. Dr. Reddy received B.Sc Degree in Physics from Osmania University, India, M.Sc (Tech) Degree in Applied Geophysics from Andhra University, India, and PhD Degree in Meteorology from Poona University, India. Dr. Reddy is survived with his wife Remata Satyavathi Reddy, two sons and one daughter and son-in-law and five grand children.

Printed in the United States
By Bookmasters